# Sometimes I Worry...

By Alan Gross
Illustrated by Mike Venezia

 CHILDRENS PRESS, CHICAGO

**Library of Congress Cataloging in Publication Data**

Gross, Allan. 1947-
  Sometimes I Worry.

    SUMMARY: Expresses common fears such as being
separated from a family or never growing and
suggests a way to deal with these worries.
    1. Fear in children—Juvenile literature.
[1. Fear. 2. Worry] I. Venezia, Mike.
II. Title.
BF723.F4G76    158     78-8019
ISBN 0-516-03670-X

# I worry, sometimes.

What if I never get big
and I have to be little all my life,
and go around talking to people's legs?

What if my house gets hit by lightning,
    or carried off in a flood,
    or attacked by monsters?

What if I get on the wrong bus
and end up in Alaska?
I won't know anybody up there.

What if nobody likes me,
    and nobody asks me to their
    birthday party,
    or sends me a valentine?

What if I tear my pants,
or spill stuff,
or break something—
something expensive?

# What if I lose my mother in a big store?

# What if there are ghosts
# in the basement?

What if big kids beat me up,
  take my money,
  steal my bike?

What if I get sick
   and can't go out to play,
   and have to stay in bed all the time?

What if I get kidnapped by Martians?
Who will rescue me?
Will they know where to look?

# What if nobody picks me
# for their team?

What if people are chasing me?
What if they think I'm a spy?

What if I swallow my gum
and a great big gum tree
grows in my stomach?

What if someone
   finds out my secrets?
Oh no.
I couldn't look at anybody then.

What if all the lions
   get out of their cages and
   eat everybody up?

# What if somebody sees me naked?

What if the train falls off the track,
   or the elevator falls all the way into
   the basement,
   or the bridge falls into the river?

# What if my family moved away
## and didn't take me with them?

21

What if my parents get divorced?
Will they still love me?
What would happen to me?

One day, my cousin told me
that he saw a kid who didn't
have any hair on his head.

"What if I lose my hair?" he said.

"Wow," I said. "Do you worry
about that stuff, too?"

"Yeah," he said. "But I almost
never tell anyone about it."

"Me too," I said. "I never tell."

One morning I asked my dad,
"What if I go bald?"

"So what?" he said. "We'd still
love you."

I told him I worried about it,
    going bald.

He told me he worried about it,
    going bald, too.

And he showed me where his hair
    was growing thin.

But I'd still love him,
  even if he was bald.

I told him I worried about
  a lot of stuff.

He asked me to tell him
  about the stuff.

I told him I couldn't.
I just couldn't.

He told me you gotta talk about
  the stuff you're worried about.

You gotta trust your friends and
  family. You gotta talk stuff out.

What if
  I get lost,

  and never
    get home,

and wander
  around forever,

  and I begin
    to starve. . . .

"What'll I do then, huh?"

What if
I get fired,

and never get
another job,

and wander
around forever,

and my family
begins to starve . . .

"What'll I do then, huh?"

And we laughed, 'cause when you share
a worry with someone who loves you
it doesn't seem so bad.

So I promised never to
keep stuff inside anymore.

But I'm worried.
What if I can't keep my promise?

"WHAT THEN, HUH?"

MIKE

ALAN

ABOUT THE AUTHOR AND ARTIST:

Alan Gross and Mike Venezia first met in 1970 while writing and designing television commercials for the Pillsbury Doughboy. They have also joined forces for Nestles Chocolate and many of the Kellogg's cereal brands. Both are native Chicagoans with solid backgrounds in children's advertising—good children's advertising, that is.

Alan, the writer, studied journalism and creative writing at the University of Missouri. He dropped out of graduate school to be an actor. Two of his plays have been produced in Chicago, *Lunching* and *The Phone Room*.

Mike, the illustrator, graduated from The School of the Art Institute in Chicago. His paintings have been shown in various galleries around Chicago.

*"Sometimes I Worry . . . "* is their first joint venture, and to tell the truth, they're a little worried.